Weekly Reader Books presents

# D.J. MACAW'S JOKE BOOK

by Mary Ellen Sias

illustrated by Jim Kersell

Weekly Reader Books

Middletown, Connecticut

This book is a presentation of Weekly Reader Books.
Weekly Reader Books offers book clubs for children
from preschool through junior high school.

For further information write to:
**Weekly Reader Books**
4343 Equity Drive
Columbus, Ohio 43228

Weekly Reader Books offers several exciting
card and activity programs. For information,
write to WEEKLY READER BOOKS, P.O. Box 16636
Columbus, Ohio 43216.

# CONTENTS

# INTRODUCTION

Hi there, friends!

I just can't stop SQUAWK-K-KING and flapping my wings about my super new joke book. I'm always jabbering about something. But what I like to jabber about most is jokes. Jokes like this one:

**Why am I never hungry at the beach?**
**Because of all the *sand — which is* there!**
**SQUAWKKKK!**

Now turn the page for more jokes. There are animal jokes and monster jokes. There are school jokes and silly riddles. There are even bird jokes — SQUAWKKKK!

You're in for a *beak* full of giggles and a SQUAWK-K-KING good time!

> Happy Chuckles!
> Love,
>         D.J. MACAW

# 1
# SCHOOL JOKES

**D. J.:** How have you been doing in school?

**John:** Well, I've been working hard to get ahead.

**D. J.:** That's good. You could certainly use one—SQUAWKKK!!

᠅

**Mother:** Becky, what are you crying about?

**Becky:** My teacher was yelling at me for something I didn't do.

**Mother:** What didn't you do?

**Becky:** My homework!

᠅

**Teacher:** D. J., what are bacteria?

**D. J.:** The back entrance to the cafeteria?

**D. J.:**    Why did you get such a low grade on your test today, Jeff?

**Jeff:**    Because the kid who always sits next to me wasn't here today.

⇥⇤

**Teacher:**  D.J., you can't sleep in my class.

**D.J.:**    I could if you didn't talk so loudly.

**Father Macaw:**  D. J., what does this *F* on your report card mean?

**D. J.:**    "Fantastic."


**Teacher:**  John, why is it so difficult for you to learn how to spell?

**John:**    Because every week you change the words.

8

**Steve:** I just found out my mother's going to night school.

**Chris:** Why did she decide to do that?

**Steve:** I'm not sure. I guess because she wants to learn to read in the dark.

⋇⋇

**Teacher:** Can you tell me how many months have 28 days in them?

**D. J.:** Of course—all of them.

⋇⋇

**Teacher:** D. J., how did they ship skeletons in the Old West?

**D. J.:** By Bony Express??

⋇⋇

**Teacher:** D. J., I thought I told you I never wanted to see you walk into this classroom late again.

**D. J.:** I know. That's why I'm crawling in.

⋇⋇

**Teacher:** D. J., what is the longest word in the English language?

**D. J.:** Smiles.

**Teacher:** Why do you say that?

**D. J.:** Because there is a whole mile between the first and the last *S*.

9

**Teacher:** Why is that pickle behind your left ear?

**D. J.:** Oh, no! I must have eaten my pencil for lunch.

>!-!<

**Teacher:** I asked you to draw a horse and wagon but you've drawn only a horse.

**D.J.:** I know. I figured the horse would draw the wagon.

**Teacher:** Kathy, why were the Indians the first people in North America?

**Kathy:** Because they had reservations??

**Mark:** Why weren't you in school today, D.J.?

**D.J.:** I had a toothache so I went to the dentist.

**Mark:** Does your tooth still ache?

**D.J.:** I don't know. The dentist kept it.

---

**Robin:** Why does the Statue of Liberty stand in New York harbor?

**Kim:** I don't know. Why?

**Robin:** Because it can't sit down.

---

**D.J.:** My teacher told me she didn't understand how one person could make so many mistakes on his homework.

**Chris:** What did you say?

**D.J.:** I told him it wasn't one person. My dad helped me.

---

**D.J.:** The other day I asked my dad if he could write in the dark.

**Robin:** What did he say?

**D.J.:** He said he thought so. So I asked him please to turn off the lights and sign my report card.

11

## 2
# ANIMAL JOKES

**D.J.:**   Which animal would you put
against your door so nobody would
open it?

**Becky:**   I don't know. Which?

**D.J.:**   A seal.

≥⌁⌁≈

**Becky:**   What kind of fish goes best with
peanut butter?

**Beth:**   I know—jellyfish.

≥⌁⌁≈

**D.J.:**   Do you know what one flea said to
the other flea?

**Kathy:**   What?

**D.J.:**   "Do you want to walk or shall we
grab the nearest dog?"

**Jeff:** I saw something yesterday that was black and white and red all over.

**John:** What was it?

**Jeff:** It was a sunburned zebra.

**D.J.:** Hey, Robin! I know a cricket that owns a rabbit. Do you know what he calls it?

**Robin:** No, what?

**D.J.:** A bug's bunny—SQUAWWWWK!

**Becky:** I just found out why my dog is such a good watchdog.

**Beth:** Why is he?

**Becky:** Because he's full of ticks.

13

**Jeff:** When the farmer grabbed the pig by the end of its tail, what did it squeal?

**Becky:** What?

**Jeff:** "I think this is the end of me."

**D.J.:** I saw a skinny horse the other day.

**Jeff:** What did it look like?

**D.J.:** A bony pony.

**Mark:** Do you know what has four legs and a tail and carries a big trunk?

**Chris:** Sure, an elephant.

**Mark:** No. It's a mouse going on a long trip.

**Robin:** After the leopard ate a hot dog for lunch, what did he say?

**Kathy:** That just hit the spot.

※

**John:** I just found a horseshoe.

**D.J.:** Do you know what that means?

**John:** No, what?

**D.J.:** Some poor horse is galloping around in his stocking feet.

※

**D.J.:** The other day Steve's dog started chewing up the newspaper.

**Mark:** What did you do?

**D.J.:** I just took the words right out of his mouth.

※

**Kim:** When a pig is sick, what kind of medicine do you use?

**Kathy:** Oinkment??

※

**D.J.:** The other day I saw a chicken throw an egg at the farmer.

**Beth:** What happened?

**D.J.:** The chicken shouted, "Now, the yolk's on you!"

**Becky:** How do you stop a skunk from smelling?

**Beth:** I don't know. How?

**Becky:** You hold his nose.

※

**D.J.:** What's green, fuzzy, and goes "squawk, squawk?"

**Mark:** What?

**D.J.:** A moldy parrot.

※

**Kim:** Kathy, do you know what cows like as their favorite food?

**Kathy:** No, what?

**Kim:** Cow chow.

※

**D.J.:** Hey, John, why didn't the horse run out of the barn?

**John:** Why?

**D.J.:** Because it was *stall*ed.

※

**Becky:** Beth, I just found out why hens lay eggs.

**Beth:** Why?

**Becky:** Because if they dropped them, they'd break!

## 3
# FOOD JOKES

**D.J.:**   Jeff, do you know what kind of flour they make Lassie's biscuits from?

**Jeff:**   No, what kind?

**D.J.:**   Collie flour—SQUAWWWK!

**Kathy:**   What makes a doughnut like a tooth?

**Kim:**   I don't know. What?

**Kathy:**   Neither one is very good without a filling.

**Chris:**   Do you know what a pancake is called that can't be eaten?

**D.J.:**   A *flop*jack???

**John:** What did one box of cereal say to the other box?

**Jeff:** What?

**John:** "Are you some kind of flake?"

>!-!<

**Steve:** Waiter, please stop slapping that margarine on my arm.

**Waiter:** But didn't you say you wanted some pats of butter??

**Mark:** A monster's dessert is always the same. Do you know what it is?

**Steve:** What?

**Mark:** Ice scream.

18

| | |
|---|---|
| **D.J.:** | If you were a sheep, what would your favorite fruit be? |
| **Kathy:** | I didn't know sheep liked fruit. |
| **D.J.:** | Yes, they love BAA-nanas. |

<br>

| | |
|---|---|
| **Kim:** | Where do you like to eat along the highway? |
| **Kathy:** | Wherever there's a fork in the road. |

<br>

| | |
|---|---|
| **D.J.:** | Have you ever watched a turkey eat its food? |
| **Jeff:** | No, how does it eat? |
| **D.J.:** | It gobbles everything in sight. |

<br>

| | |
|---|---|
| **Kathy:** | Do you know why one strawberry called the other one for help? |
| **Kim:** | Why? |
| **Kathy:** | Because it was in a real jam. |

<br>

| | |
|---|---|
| **D.J.:** | Knock, knock. |
| **Steve:** | Who's there? |
| **D.J.:** | Lettuce. |
| **Steve:** | Lettuce who? |
| **D.J.:** | Lettuce in. |

19

**Robin:** What did one pickle call the other one who was acting funny?

**Kathy:** What?

**Robin:** "You silly dilly."

><_><_

**D.J.:** Knock, knock.

**Jeff:** Who's there?

**D.J.:** Catsup.

**Jeff:** Catsup who?

**D.J.:** *Catsup* a tree!

><_><_

**Beth:** D.J., what kind of a train is always carrying gum?

**D.J.:** Let me guess. A chew-chew train?

><_><_

**John:** Do you know how to make an apple turnover?

**Jeff:** No. How?

**John:** You just tickle it.

><_><_

**D.J.:** I eat a lot of carrots because they're good for my eyes.

**Chris:** How do you know that?

**D.J.:** Have you ever seen a rabbit wearing glasses?

**D.J.:** Two potato chips were walking near a pool. What did one say to the other?

**Mark:** What?

**D.J.:** "Want to go for a dip?"

**D.J.:** Kim, what do you get if you cross a potato with an onion?

**Kim:** I don't know. What?

**D.J.:** A potato with very watery eyes.

**Teacher:** Can you tell us where the very first doughnut was made?

**D.J.:** Of course. In Greece.

# 4
# MONSTER JOKES

**Kathy:** What do ghosts chew?
**Kim:** What?
**Kathy:** Boo-ble gum.

**D.J.:** What's the first thing ghosts say
when I ride in their cars?
**Mark:** What?
**D.J.:** "Fasten your sheet belt."

**Becky:** When witches are on their
broomsticks, how do they drink
their tea?
**Beth:** I don't know. How?
**Becky:** Out of flying saucers.

**D.J.:** What did Count Dracula say when he stopped biting my neck?

**Mark:** What?

**D.J.:** "It's been nice gnawing you."

**D.J.:** When I spoke to a two-headed monster yesterday, he sounded a lot like me.

**Becky:** Why? What did he say?

**D.J.:** Hello, hello. How are you? How are you?

23

**D.J.:** When the ghost haunted the dairy farm, what did the cows get?

**John:** What?

**D.J.:** Milk shakes.

**Jeff:** What did the witch ask for in the hotel?

**Beth:** What?

**Jeff:** *Broom* service.

**Robin:** Who sits in the front of the room in a monster school?

**Mark:** Who?

**Robin:** The creature teacher.

**D.J.:** I can never believe what Count Dracula says when he's in his coffin resting.

**Steve:** Why?

**D.J.:** Because he's always lying.

**D.J.:** What kind of beans does a monster like best?

**Beth:** What kind?

**D.J.:** Human beans.

**Jeff:** Where is a vampire's favorite tourist place?

**Chris:** Where?

**Jeff:** The Vampire State Building.

>ι-ι<

**D.J.:** What would you get if you crossed a mummy and a parrot?

**John:** What?

**D.J.:** A gift-wrapped bird—SQUAWWWK!

25

**D.J.:** If you crossed a werewolf with a parrot, what would you get?

**Kathy:** What?

**D.J.:** A fur collar that doesn't stop talking—SQUAWKKK!!

※※※

**Mark:** What is a vampire's toothache called?

**Steve:** I don't know. What?

**Mark:** A fang pang.

※※※

**D.J.:** How did the fire-eating dragon burn his fingers?

**Jeff:** How?

**D.J.:** He put his hand over his mouth when he sneezed.

※※※

**D.J.:** What kind of plant did the witch like in my back yard?

**Kathy:** What kind?

**D.J.:** Poison ivy.

※※※

**D.J.:** What song does the ghost love to sing to me?

**John:** What?

**D.J.:** "A-Haunting We Will Go."

26

# 5
# SPORTS JOKES

**Kathy:** Do you know how all the basketball players keep cool at the games?

**Kim:** No, how?

**Kathy:** All of their fans are there.

>!-!<

**Chris:** John, do you know how the athlete sprained himself at the Olympics?

**John:** No, how?

**Chris:** He slipped his discus.

>!-!<

**Jeff:** Why is it hard to drive golf balls?

**John:** Why?

**Jeff:** Because they don't have steering wheels.

**D.J.:** The football player wanted to go to the movies. So he asked his coach for eight thousand dollars.

**Kathy:** Why?

**D.J.:** Because he wanted to go to a drive-in and he didn't have a car.

**D.J.:** How many successful jumps does a skydiver have to make before he gets his diploma?

**Beth:** How many?

**D.J.:** All of them.

**Kim:** How does a baseball player hold his bat?

**Kathy:** How?

**Kim:** By its wings.

*※*

**D.J.:** Do you know why a good golfer always wears two pair of pants?

**Mark:** No, why?

**D.J.:** Just in case he gets a hole in one.

*※*

**D.J.:** Why don't hippos play basketball?

**Steve:** Why?

**D.J.:** They don't look good in shorts.

*※*

**Mark:** Why do spiders play the outfield in baseball games?

**John:** I don't know. Why?

**Mark:** Because they're good at catching flies.

*※*

**Robin:** Why is a bad golfer a lot like a bad toaster?

**Kim:** Why?

**Robin:** Because they both need to correct their slice.

**Becky:** When you're a jogger, how do you avoid that "run-down" feeling?

**Beth:** How?

**Becky:** You look both ways before you cross the street.

>!~!~

**D.J.:** In what way is boating like a department store?

**Steve:** What way?

**D.J.:** They both do best when they have a sail.

>!~!~

**Becky:** How is a good golfer like a doughnut?

**Beth:** How?

**Becky:** They both have a hole in one.

**D.J.:**   My bicycle will never go as fast as my car.

**Steve:**  Why not?

**D.J.:**   It's always two-tired.

⋊⦙⋉

**John:**   Athletes often have athlete's foot. Do you know what astronauts often have?

**Jeff:**   No, what?

**John:**   Would you believe, missile toes?

⋊⦙⋉

**Chris:**  What kind of car do you think a golfer's helper drives?

**Steve:**  What kind?

**Chris:**  A Caddie-lac.

⋊⦙⋉

**D.J.:**   A karate blow is like a piece of meat.

**Becky:**  Why do you say that?

**D.J.:**   Because it's a real poke chop.

⋊⦙⋉

**John:**   The other day I saw a fish that weighed 20 pounds jump out of the water.

**Jeff:**   How did you know that?

**John:**   Because of all the scales on its back.

31

# 6
## FAMILY JOKES

**Mother**
**Macaw:** D.J., eat all your spinach so you'll have beautiful colored cheeks.
**D.J.:** Why? I don't want green cheeks.

>⟶⟵

**Beth:** Mommy, I've been trying to help you.
**Mommy:** How have you helped me?
**Beth:** I licked all the stamps and they're ready to put on all your letters now.

>⟶⟵

**Mark:** Dad, will you buy me a bike?
**Dad:** Mark, you're too old for a bike.
**Mark:** O.K. Then why don't you make it a car?

**Kim:** I noticed the other day that my little brother had written *TGIF* on his sneakers.

**Kathy:** What did that mean?

**Kim:** He said it meant "toes go in first."

**Father Macaw:** There's something wrong with my shaving brush.

**D.J.:** That's funny — it worked perfectly yesterday, when I painted my bike.

**Mother Macaw:** D.J., there were two pieces of cake on the table last night. This morning I see only one.

**D.J.:** I don't know what happened. I guess I didn't see the other piece in the dark.

*⋇*

**Mother Macaw:** D.J., how come you are always getting into so much more trouble than the other boys?

**D.J.:** I don't know. Maybe it's because you make me get up so much earlier.

*⋇*

**John:** My baby brother finally ate all his oatmeal.

**Jeff:** Why did he suddenly do that?

**John:** Because I told him it was mud.

*⋇*

**Steve:** We have lots of new controls on our TV set.

**Chris:** We have only four.

**Steve:** Why only four?

**Chris:** There's my father, my mother, and my two sisters.

**Steve:** D.J., what time is it?

**D.J.:** I'm not sure, but I know it's not five o'clock yet.

**Steve:** How do you know?

**D.J.:** Because I have to be home at five o'clock and I'm not there yet.

**Mother Macaw:** D.J., why do you always get so dirty?

**D.J.:** Mom, I'm always closer to the ground than you are.

**Father Macaw:** D.J., your report card is not good. We know you're not a slow learner.

**D.J.:** I know. But I'm a fast forgetter.

# 7
# SILLY RIDDLES

Where does D.J. take his watch if it is sick?
*To a tick doc.*

Why does D.J. always wear boots in a pet store?
*Because he might step in a poodle.*

What did the tomato say to the kid who was running behind him?
*Catsup.*

How does D.J. lift his heavy duck friend?
*With a quacker jack.*

What is white, small, fluffy, and barks?
*Pupcorn.*

Why did D.J. put on a wet shirt?
*Because it said "Wash and Wear."*

≥!-⁄←

Why does D.J. always fly south?
*Because it's too far to walk.*

≥!-⁄←

What did the bees say when D.J. asked them why they were always humming?
*"We don't know the words."*

≥!-⁄←

Why did D.J. put his radio in the refrigerator?
*He wanted to hear cool music.*

What does D.J. call a lion who eats ice cubes?
*A cool cat.*

What colors did D.J. paint the sun and the wind?

> *He painted the sun rose and the wind blew.*

>⅊⅃⅄⅂

How did D.J. catch the squirrel?

> *He ran up the tree and acted like a nut.*

What do you call a small joke?

> *A mini-ha-ha.*

What did the waiter say when D.J. asked if they served crabs in the restaurant?

> *"Yes, we serve anyone here, sir."*

What do you get when you cross a giraffe
with a rooster?
*An animal that can awaken people on the
very top floor.*

⋙—⋘

What did D.J. have when he crossed a mink
with an octopus?
*A fur coat with too many sleeves.*

⋙—⋘

What did D.J. say to the locksmith when
his house caught on fire?
*"Make a bolt for the door!"*

⋙—⋘

How did D.J. begin his book about ducks?
*With an intro-duck-tion!*

⋙—⋘

How did D.J. help his sick bird friend?
*He gave him first-aid tweetment.*

⋙—⋘

What kind of vegetable is red and brown?
*A tomato with lots of freckles.*

⋙—⋘

What do you get when you cross a
telephone and a shirt?
*A ring around the collar.*

Why did D.J. get a zero on his spelling test?
*He didn't. The teacher ran out of stars so she gave him a moon.*

⋍⃜

A moon is always going to the bank. Why?
*To change quarters.*

⋍⃜

Where did D.J. say he could always find money?
*In his dictionary.*

⋍⃜

What did D.J. call the baby kangaroo who was always on the lookout?
*A pocket watch.*

⋍⃜

What did the envelope say when D.J. licked it?
*Nothing. It just shut up.*

⋍⃜

What did D.J. say when asked why his beak was in the middle of his face?
*"Because it's my scenter." SQUAWWWK!*

⋍⃜

Why can't anyone understand zippers?
*They only talk in zip code.*

⋍⃜

How did the rocket lose its job?
*It ended up being fired.*

40